DK Penguin Random House

Senior Editors Daniel Mills, Alka Ranjan, Fleur Star, Bharti Bedi
Senior Art Editors Vicky Short, Mahua Sharma
Editors Susmita Dey, Neha Pande
Art Editors Sanjay Chauhan, Rakesh Khundongbam, Vaibhav Rastogi, Priyanka Bansal
US Editor Margaret Parrish
Picture Researcher Ashwin Raju Adimari
Senior DTP Designer Harish Aggarwal
DTP Designers Arvind Kumar, Pawan Kumar
Jacket Designer Dhirendra Singh
Pre-production Producer Jacqueline Street
Production Controller Ed Kneafsey
Pre-production Manager Balwant Singh
Production Manager Pankaj Sharma
Picture Research Manager Taiyaba Khatoon
Managing Editors Paula Regan, Francesca Baines, Rohan Sinha, Kingshuk Ghoshal
Managing Art Editors Owen Peyton Jones, Philip Letsu, Govind Mittal
Deputy Managing Art Editor Sudakshina Basu
Publishers Sarah Larter, Andrew Macintyre
Art Directors Phil Ormerod, Karen Self
Associate Publishing Director Liz Wheeler
Publishing Director Jonathan Metcalf
Special Sales and Custom Publishing Manager Michelle Baxter
Author David Burnie

Content previously published as *The Animal Book* in 2013

First American Edition, 2017
Published in the United States by DK Publishing,
345 Hudson Street, New York, New York 10014

Copyright © 2017 Dorling Kindersley Limited
DK, a Division of Penguin Random House LLC
17 18 19 20 21 10 9 8 7 6 5 4 3 2
001—308419—July/17

A catalog record for this book is available from the Library of Congress.
ISBN: 978-5-0010-1469-0

DK books are available at special discounts when purchased in bulk for sales promotions, premiums, fund-raising, or educational use. For details, contact: DK Publishing Special Markets, 345 Hudson Street, New York, New York 10014 SpecialSales@dk.com
Printed and bound in China

A WORLD OF IDEAS:
SEE ALL THERE IS TO KNOW

www.dk.com

Smithsonian Institution
THE SMITHSONIAN

Established in 1846, the Smithsonian—the world's largest museum and research complex—includes 19 museums and galleries and the National Zoological Park. The total number of artifacts, works of art, and specimens in the Smithsonian's collection is estimated at 137 million, the bulk of which is contained in the National Museum of Natural History. The National Zoo has more than 4,000 animals in its living collection. The Smithsonian is a renowned research center, dedicated to public education, national service, and scholarship in the arts, sciences, and history.

AMPHIBIANS AND REPTILES

Contents

Frilled lizard

Throughout this book you will find scale boxes that show the sizes of living creatures compared to you.

Child = 57 in (145 cm) tall

Hand = 6 in (16 cm) long

Thumb = 1 1/3 in (3.5 cm) long

Amphibians

Amphibians spend part of their lives in the water and part on land. Some kinds undergo metamorphosis, like many invertebrates, starting out as water-based tadpoles with gills and evolving into air-breathing adults. They need freshwater to survive, and many species are threatened with extinction due to pollution, disease, and destruction of their habitats.

Yellow banded poison-dart frog

Skin › Amphibians have permeable skin, so water can pass outward and evaporate. Becuase of this, they mostly live in water or in damp areas to keep their bodies from drying out.

Poison glands ❯ Many species of amphibian secrete a poisonous slime from glands in their skin. This helps to keep them moist and deter predators. Some amphibians simply taste nasty, while others, like this yellow banded poison-dart frog, can be deadly to some predators.

Features

- Usually lay eggs to reproduce

- Have moist skin and may die if they dry out

- Often spend much of their lives in water

- Some hatch as tadpoles and change shape to become adults

- Are cold-blooded

Legs ❯ Some amphibians only have legs as adults. These kinds hatch out from eggs as tadpoles, tiny swimming creatures with tails. As the tadpoles mature, legs grow out of their bodies and their tails shrink and disappear.

Frogs and toads

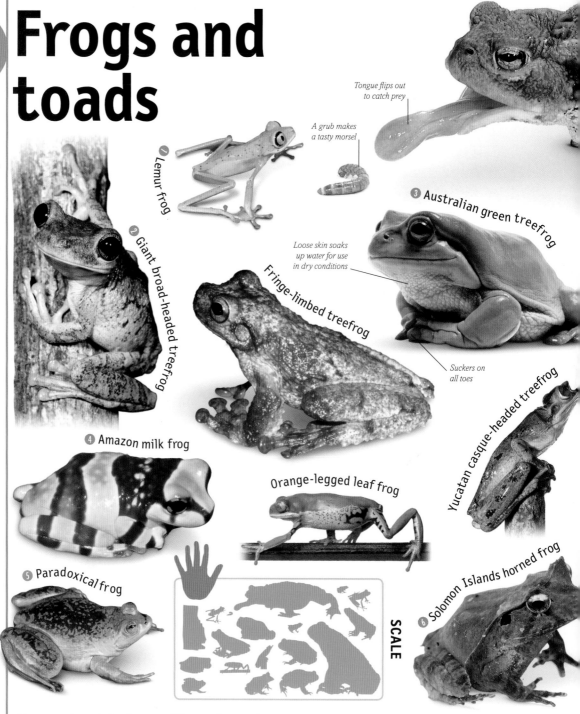

Tongue flips out to catch prey

A grub makes a tasty morsel

① Lemur frog

③ Australian green treefrog

② Giant broad-headed treefrog

Loose skin soaks up water for use in dry conditions

Fringe-limbed treefrog

Suckers on all toes

④ Amazon milk frog

Orange-legged leaf frog

Yucatan casque-headed treefrog

⑤ Paradoxical frog

SCALE

⑥ Solomon Islands horned frog

Frogs and toads look very different from other amphibians, with their stubby bodies and long back legs. Frogs are usually sleek and slippery, but most toads have dry, warty skin. Nearly all of these animals start life as tadpoles, changing shape as they grow up. The **lemur frog** ❶ from Central America hunts insects by night and hides under leaves during the day. Like other treefrogs, it is an expert

climber with slender, sucker-tipped toes. The **giant broad-headed treefrog** ❷ lives in South American forests. It clings to tree trunks and branches, while the **Australian green treefrog** ❸ sometimes climbs into houses, where it makes itself at home in water tanks and kitchen sinks. The **Amazon milk frog** ❹ lays its eggs in rain-filled tree-holes. It lives high in the treetops and hardly ever comes to the

7 European common toad

8 Golden mantella

Elegant Madagascan frog

Guyanan stubfoot toad

Eyes with slit-shaped pupils detect small, moving prey

9 Malayan tree toad

10 Cane toad

Raucous toad

Warts on male's skin develop dark, sharp spines in the breeding season

Natterjack toad

ground. The South American **paradoxical frog** **5** spends its life in lakes and pools. It gets its name from its monster tadpoles, which are up to four times the adult's length. The **Solomon Islands horned frog** **6** has a pointed snout and hornlike projections above its eyes, camouflaging it perfectly among fallen leaves. The **European common toad** **7** hunts all kinds of small animals, including beetles, snails, and slugs.

The rare **golden mantella** **8** frog from Madagascar is brilliantly colored, warning predators that it has poison-covered skin. The **Malayan tree toad** **9** is one of the few true toads that lives off the ground. The enormous **cane toad** **10** gulps down mice and even snakes. Originally from Central America, this ravenous predator has become a major pest in Australia and other parts of the world.

Common parsley frog

Brazil-nut poison-dart frog

⑪ European common frog

⑬ Granular poison-dart frog

⑫ Golden poison-dart frog

Yellow-banded poison-dart frog

Dyeing poison-dart frog

Circular eardrums behind eyes

Three-striped poison-dart frog

⑭ Edible frog

⑯ American bullfrog

⑮ Wood frog

SCALE

Tungara frog

Toads usually move by crawling, but frogs often hop and jump. In emergencies, the **European common frog** ⑪ can leap more than seven times its own length, equivalent to a human athlete clearing a school bus without a run-up. In Central and South America, tiny poison-dart frogs climb up trees or hop over the rain-forest floor. Their bright colors are a warning to predators to stay

away. The **golden poison-dart frog** ⑫ is the deadliest, with enough poison to kill two African elephants, while the **granular poison-dart frog** ⑬ is one of the smallest and could easily fit inside a matchbox. In the past, Native Americans used these frogs to make poison hunting darts, which is how they got their names. In the breeding season, frogs and toads often make loud calls. Male **edible frogs** ⑭

17 Asian horned frog

18 Indian bullfrog

Bolifamba reed frog

Giant stump-toed frog

Common skittering frog

19 Painted toad

Rajamally wart frog

Sticky, bright red skin to ward off predators

Couch's spadefoot

Foulassi banana frog

21 Tinker reed frog

20 Tomato frog

and **wood frogs** 15 sound like quacking ducks, while the male **American bullfrog** 16 sounds more like a mooing cow. This massive frog swallows almost anything it can cram into its mouth, including smaller frogs, young turtles, and small water birds. The "horns" and the brown color of the **Asian horned frog** 17 help it blend in among fallen leaves. The **Indian bullfrog** 18 leaps into water if it is disturbed.

It usually climbs out after a few minutes, but can stay underwater for several hours. **Painted toads** 19 and **tomato frogs** 20 live on land and come out to feed at night. Their skin is covered with a gluelike substance, which helps to protect them from attack. **Tinker reed frogs** 21 from Africa lay their eggs on waterside plants. Their tadpoles wriggle down into the water after hatching.

㉒ Mexican burrowing toad

Spotted-thighed poison-dart frog

SCALE

Oriental fire-bellied toad

㉓ Horned marsupial frog

painted frog

Eggs wrapped around male's hind legs

㉕ Fleischmann's glass frog

㉔ Midwife toad

Mouth as wide as head

㉖ Ornate horned frog

Big-headed rain frog

Mascarene ridged frog

Frogs and toads have lots of different shapes and varied lifestyles that help them to survive. If threatened, the **Mexican burrowing toad** ㉒ can blow itself up to resemble a small balloon. It lives underground and feeds on ants, coming to the surface only when it breeds. The **horned marsupial frog** ㉓ has a strange way of breeding that lets it stay high up in trees. The female carries her eggs in a pouch on her back. Instead of producing tadpoles, they hatch directly into baby frogs. The **midwife toad** ㉔ was so named because the male carries the female's eggs. When the eggs are ready to hatch, he takes them to water so that the tadpoles can swim away. **Fleischmann's glass frog** ㉕ lives in trees. On its underside, its tiny beating heart can be seen through its transparent skin. The **ornate horned frog** ㉖ is a sit-and-

African foam-nest treefrog

Darwin's frog

Webbed feet work like parachutes

Coromandel New Zealand frog

㉗ Desert rain frog

Mossy frog

Southern whipping frog

㉘ Wallace's flying frog

African treefrog

West Cameroon forest treefrog

Puerto Rican coqui

Brown-striped marsh frog

㉙ Fraser's clawed frog

Limon robber frog

㉛ Common spadefoot toad

㉚ African bullfrog

wait hunter from the grasslands of Argentina. Camouflaged by its green and brown markings, it lurks in muddy ground and grabs anything edible that comes nearby. The **desert rain frog** ㉗ lives and breeds among Namibian sand dunes, hiding beneath the surface during the day. **Wallace's flying frog** ㉘ glides through the forests of Southeast Asia on its webbed feet. **Fraser's clawed frog** ㉙ from Africa

stays in water all its life. It has a flat body, sensitive fingers, and upward-facing eyes. The **African bullfrog** ㉚ lives in grassland and savanna. Big and aggressive, it sometimes eats its own kind. It spends the dry season underground. Males of this species defend their eggs fiercely until they hatch. The **common spadefoot toad** ㉛ digs burrows with its back legs and spends half the year hidden away.

Salamanders and newts

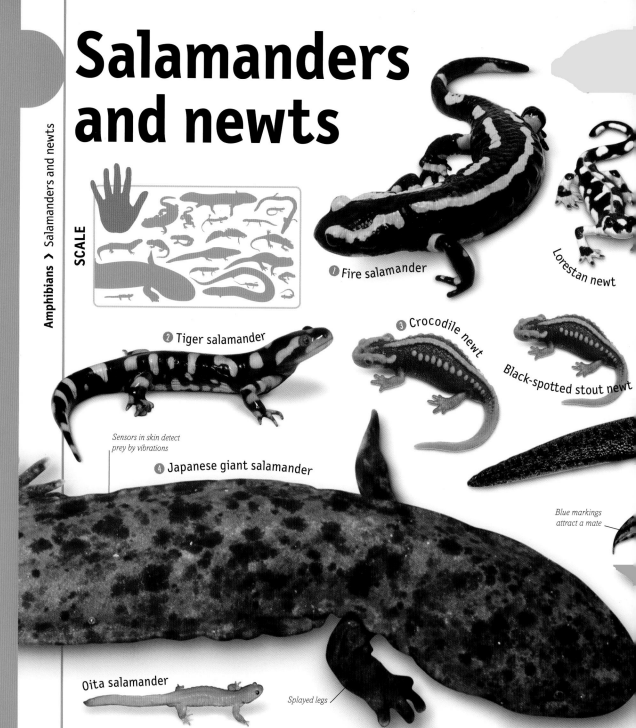

SCALE

❶ Fire salamander

Lorestan newt

❷ Tiger salamander

❸ Crocodile newt

Black-spotted stout newt

Sensors in skin detect prey by vibrations

❹ Japanese giant salamander

Blue markings attract a mate

Oita salamander

Splayed legs

With their slender bodies and long tails, salamanders and newts look very different from frogs and toads. Many are well camouflaged, but others, including the **fire salamander** ❶ and **tiger salamander** ❷, have bright warning colors. This shows other animals that they are poisonous and best left alone. Some species spend all their lives on land, but most return to water to mate and lay their eggs. The Asian **crocodile newt** ❸ heads for ponds at the beginning of the monsoon, while the **Japanese giant salamander** ❹ is fully aquatic and never leaves its watery home. Measuring up to 5 ft (1.5 m) long, this huge, wrinkly-skinned amphibian feeds on fish and freshwater insects and hunts after dark. Young salamanders and newts breathe using feathery gills. Some salamander species, such as the

⑤ Axolotl

Feathery gills

Three-lined salamander

⑥ Olm

Sardinian brook salamander

Italian cave salamander

⑦ Great crested newt

⑧ California newt

Sharp-ribbed salamander

Bones can poke through sides for defence

California giant salamander

Alpine newt

⑨ Ensatina salamander

Spectacled salamander

⑩ Three-toed amphiuma

Four-toed salamander

axolotl ⑤ and **olm** ⑥, keep their gills throughout their lives. If the axolotl loses a body part, it can regrow the entire part within months. The olm lives in dark, flooded caves. Extremely slender and totally blind, it finds its food by smell and touch. **Great crested newts** ⑦ breed in ponds and have elaborate courtship displays. The male grows his impressive crest in spring and uses it to attract females waiting to lay their eggs.

On land, salamanders and newts live in damp woodlands and rocky places, and they hunt mainly after dark. During the summer, many species, such as the **California newt** ⑧ and **Ensatina salamander** ⑨, keep moist by hiding under rotting logs. The **three-toed amphiuma** ⑩ buries itself in mud and makes a waterproof cocoon. This slimy, snakelike amphibian has tiny legs but a powerful bite.

Reptiles

Millions of years ago reptiles ruled the Earth in the form of dinosaurs. Modern reptiles are mostly smaller, although they still include fearsome predators such as the Komodo dragon, giant snakes, and ferocious crocodiles, which can attack and kill human beings. However, they also include gentle vegetarians, such as giant tortoises and the green sea turtle.

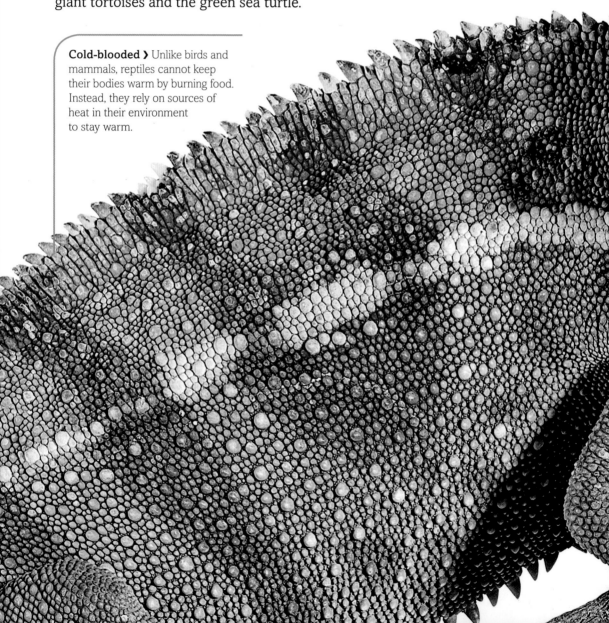

Cold-blooded ❯ Unlike birds and mammals, reptiles cannot keep their bodies warm by burning food. Instead, they rely on sources of heat in their environment to stay warm.

Scaly skin ❯ In addition to skin, reptiles have an outer layer of protective armor. Lizards and snakes are covered in scales. Turtles, tortoises, crocodiles, and alligators have scutes, which are horny layers of skin backed by bony plates.

Features

- Most lay eggs to reproduce

- Have dry, scaly skin

- Most are meat-eaters

- Most live in warmer climates

- Are cold-blooded

Panther chameleon

Lungs ❯ Reptiles have lungs and must breathe air to survive. Even turtles that live underwater usually return to the surface to breathe.

Legs ❯ Most reptiles have four legs. Some groups, such as snakes, have no legs at all. They move by pushing against the ground with their flexible bodies.

Turtles and tortoises

Blanding's turtle

Golden coin turtle

① Yellow-marginated box turtle

② Red-bellied turtle

Hawksbill sea turtle

Jaws can cut fish in two

Red-eared slider

④ Leatherback sea turtle

③ Carolina box turtle

Rubbery shell

Saltwater terrapin

⑤ Common snapping turtle

Hooked beak delivers a powerful bite

With their domed shells and beaklike mouths, turtles and tortoises are easy to recognize. The **yellow-marginated box turtle** ① has a hinge on the underside of its shell. If danger strikes, it quickly pulls in its head and legs and shuts itself away. The American **red-bellied turtle** ② likes sunning itself near the shore, while the **Carolina box turtle** ③ escapes the heat by retreating into cover or by burying itself in mud. Turtles and tortoises come in many sizes. The smallest ones are not much bigger than a baseball, but the record-breaking **leatherback sea turtle** ④ can weigh as much as a small car. It is one of the greatest travelers in the animal world, swimming vast distances with its large flippers. Sea turtles live mainly in tropical oceans, but freshwater turtles live in rivers and lakes, where they eat

Big-headed turtle

Chinese soft-shelled turtle ⑥

① Painted turtle

European pond turtle

Matamata

False map turtle

Common snake-necked turtle

Asian leaf turtle

⑧ Alligator snapping turtle

Mississippi mud turtle

Common musk turtle

Ornate box turtle

⑨ Loggerhead sea turtle

Paddlelike limb

Yellow slider

SCALE

plants or animal prey. The **common snapping turtle** ⑤, from North America, is one of the world's biggest freshwater turtles. It lurks in the mud at the bottom of rivers and lakes. The **Chinese soft-shelled turtle** ⑥ has a nose like a snorkel, and it spends most of its time in the water. Turtles and tortoises breed by laying eggs. Freshwater kinds, such as the **painted turtle** ⑦, lay theirs in holes not far from the water's edge. The

female **alligator snapping turtle** ⑧ leaves the water in the spring to lay eggs, whereas the male spends most of his time at the bottom of rivers or lakes. Sea turtles, including the **loggerhead** ⑨, dig nests in sandy beaches. After hatching, the young turtles dig their way to the surface and then scuttle toward the sea. It is a dangerous time, and many are caught by predators before they reach the water's edge.

17

SCALE

Saddle shape allows tortoise to raise its head

⑪ Hermann's tortoise

⑩ Red-footed tortoise

Sharp jaw for cutting through food

⑫ Aldabra giant tortoise

⑬ Pancake tortoise

Scales on shell show growth rings

Bowsprit tortoise

Tortoises are close relatives of turtles, but they have stronger legs and spend all their lives on land. Like turtles, tortoises breed by laying eggs. Most of them are vegetarian, although some, including the South American **red-footed tortoise** ⑩, also eat small animals and dead remains. Tortoises are famous for being slow, but to make up for this, they can be amazingly long-lived. The

Hermann's tortoise ⑪, for example, has a life span of 50 years, while the **Aldabra giant tortoise** ⑫ from coral islands in the Indian Ocean can survive for more than two centuries. One recently died in captivity at the astonishing age of 255. Most tortoises have high shells, which predators find hard to break. The African **pancake tortoise** ⑬ is almost flat, which allows it to hide in rocky cracks to avoid

⑭ Galápagos tortoise

⑮ Radiated tortoise

Shell with vertical streaks

Elongated tortoise

⑯ Indian starred tortoise

Bumpy shell

Serrated hinge-back tortoise

Wood turtle

⑰ Spur-thighed tortoise

Leopard tortoise

⑱ Desert tortoise

predators. It has the tiniest families, since it lays just one egg at a time, although it usually breeds several times each year. **Galápagos tortoises** ⑭ live on islands in the Pacific Ocean. They are as large as the Aldabra giant tortoise and often have shells with a saddle-shaped front. This lets them stretch their necks high up to munch prickly cacti, their primary food. **Radiated tortoises** ⑮, from Madagascar,

have shells with raised knobs, but the lumpiest shell belongs to the **Indian starred tortoise** ⑯, which has starlike markings that hide it in dry grass. The **spur-thighed tortoise** ⑰ from Europe and North Africa has bony projections on its hind legs. It lays up to 20 eggs at a time, while the **desert tortoise** ⑱, found in small burrows in the deserts of North America, lays as few as four eggs.

Lizards

① Emerald skink

Slender toes for climbing trees

SCALE

Green anole

Cape girdled lizard

Shiny, beadlike scales

② Gila monster

Desert horned lizard

③ Asian water monitor

④ Madagascar day gecko

Toes with sharp claws for climbing

There are more than 4,000 lizard species in the world, more than all other reptiles put together. Most of them hunt small animals, and most lay eggs, although some give birth to live young. The **emerald skink** ① preys on insects. It spends most of its time on tree trunks, while the heavy-bodied **Gila monster** ② stays on the ground. Found in North American deserts, the Gila monster is one

of the few lizards with a poisonous bite. Fortunately, it is a slow mover, so attacks on people are very rare. The fierce **Asian water monitor** ③ grows up to 6½ ft (2 m) long. A good swimmer, it hunts all kinds of animals, from fishes and frogs to crabs. The **Madagascar day gecko** ④ is mostly found on trees and belongs to a family of lizard famous for its "sticky" toes. Like other geckos, it can cling to almost any

20

⑤ Frilled lizard

Frill opens like an umbrella

⑥ Sandfish skink

Strong back legs built for speed

Long, flattened tail used in swimming

⑦ Green basilisk

Knight anole

Large psammodromus

Spiky crest

⑧ Marine iguana

Rough-scaled plated lizard

Viviparous lizard

Wonder gecko

surface, and can even hunt upside down. When faced with danger, many lizards shed their tails. This distracts their enemies while they run away. The Australian **frilled lizard** ⑤ uses a different technique to protect itself. It stands its ground and opens up its frill, making it look much more threatening than it really is. The North African **sandfish skink** ⑥ dives for safety, disappearing into the desert sand by "swimming" through it. The **green basilisk** ⑦ from Central America has the most impressive escape trick of all. Standing on its back legs, it runs over the surface of lakes and streams, before swimming away from the predator. Found in the Galápagos Islands, the **marine iguana** ⑧ is the only lizard that feeds in the sea. It uses its blunt jaws to tear seaweed from underwater rocks.

21

⑨ Common leopard gecko

⑩ Slow worm

Solomon Islands skink

⑪ Common scaly foot

Berber skink

Mediterranean gecko

⑫ Green iguana

Italian wall lizard

Moorish gecko

⑬ Parson's chameleon

Tail can wrap around branches

Colorado desert fringe-toed lizard

SCALE

Fringe-toed lizard

Geckos are widespread in warm parts of the world, where there are plenty of insects for them to hunt. One of the most popular reptile pets, the **common leopard gecko** ⑨ from South Asia is easy to care for. This small gecko has an amazingly loud call for an animal just 8 in (20 cm) long. The **slow worm** ⑩, from Europe, has no legs at all, while the **common scaly foot** ⑪, from Australia,

looks like a snake with tiny leg flaps, Both of these lizards hunt insects and spiders, finding their prey on the ground. The Central American **green iguana** ⑫ is a much bigger reptile, with a spiked crest. Although it looks dangerous, it feeds mainly on plants and often climbs high up in trees. Chameleons are even better climbers and hardly ever come to the ground. **Parson's chameleon** ⑬ from Madagascar

22

Western banded gecko

14 Tokay gecko

Yellow-spotted night lizard

Green-striped tree dragon

15 African fat-tailed gecko

Body fat in
tail used as a
food reserve

16 Jackson's chameleon

17 Red tegu

is the largest chameleon. It creeps along branches using
its feet and its tail and catches insects by shooting out its
unbelievably long, sticky tongue. Like other chameleons,
its eyes swivel in all directions, and it can change color
to match its background or to show its mood. The **tokay
gecko 14** gets its name from its harsh "to-kay" call. This
large gecko from Southeast Asia lives in houses and often

hunts indoors. **African fat-tailed geckos 15** live in deserts.
Unlike other geckos, they do not have sticky toes, and they
rarely climb. **Jackson's chameleon 16** lives in East Africa.
The males of this species are identified by the three horns
on their snouts. The **red tegu 17** is one of the biggest lizards
in South America. A predator and a scavenger, it sometimes
steals chickens from farms.

23

Snakes

SCALE

Prairie rattlesnake

① Gaboon viper

Malayan pit viper

Asp viper

Red color darkens with age

② Mole viper

Red spitting cobra

③ Desert death adder

④ Boa constrictor

Sunbeam snake

Wide scales on underside

Ceylonese pipesnake

East African sand boa

Neck widens into "hood" to scare off predators

⑤ King cobra

⑥ Monocled cobra

Rainbow boa

With their sleek, shiny bodies and needle-sharp fangs, snakes often trigger panic and fear. Most kinds are harmless to humans, but venomous ones kill more than 20,000 people a year. All snakes are legless, and nearly all eat live prey. Their amazingly flexible jaws and stomachs let them swallow animals much wider than themselves. The African **Gaboon viper** ① waits to ambush its prey with record-breaking fangs up to 2 in (5 cm) long. In a single bite, it can inject enough venom to kill a baboon or an antelope. The African **mole viper** ② catches small animals underground, while the extremely venomous **desert death adder** ③ from Australia attracts food by using the thin, wormlike tip of its tail as a lure. The **boa constrictor** ④ from Central America is nonvenomous and kills by muscle power alone. Like other

24

Western diamond-backed rattlesnake ❼

"Rattle" made of dry skin

Desert horned viper

Dusty color provides camouflage

❽ Green anaconda

Central American coral snake

❾ Eurasian blindsnake

Rosy boa

❿ Yellow-lipped seakrait

constrictors, it coils around its prey, tightening its grip while the victim slowly suffocates. Boas feed mainly on mammals and birds, but the Asian **king cobra** ❺ is an expert at eating other snakes. At 16 ft (5 m) long, it is the biggest venomous snake on Earth. The **monocled cobra** ❻ expands its neck into a "hood" when threatened, while the North American **western diamond-backed rattlesnake** ❼ makes a rattling sound with its tail to warn off enemies. The mighty **green anaconda** ❽ is one of the world's longest and heaviest snakes, weighing more than 220 lb (100 kg). At the other extreme, the **Eurasian blindsnake** ❾ is often less than 12 in (30 cm) long. It feeds on ants, spiders, and centipedes. Most snakes are good swimmers. The **yellow-lipped seakrait** ❿ spends its life in tropical waters, coming to land only when it is time to breed.

⑪ Blood python

Long-nosed snake

Banded flying snake ⑬

⑫ Green tree python

⑭ Burmese python

Balkan racer

Heat sensors in front
of eyes to detect prey

Smooth snake

⑮ California mountain kingsnake

Some snakes give birth to live young, but most breed by laying eggs. Female **blood pythons** ⑪ from Southeast Asia coil around their eggs to keep them warm. The mother stays with her eggs for up to three months and does not eat until her young have hatched. The **green tree python** ⑫ from Australasia is a superb climber, but the Asian **banded flying snake** ⑬ is even better at moving around in trees. It jumps from tree to tree, gliding up to 330 ft (100 m) by stretching out its body and flattening its underside. The **Burmese python** ⑭ is one of the longest snakes in the world, measuring up to 23 ft (7 m) from head to tail. Like all pythons and rattlesnakes, it has heat sensors on its head, letting it "see" warm-blooded prey even when it is completely dark. The brightly patterned **California**

Spotted python

⑰ Grass snake

Giant Malagasy hognose snake

Pointed snout adapted for burrowing

⑯ Pine snake

Distinctive yellow collar

Ruthven's kingsnake

Brown treesnake

False water cobra ⑱

Broad black streak behind eyes

Red-tailed green ratsnake

⑲ Garter snake

SCALE

Tail used as an anchor while climbing

mountain kingsnake ⑮ looks venomous, but its colors are a trick and it is actually nonpoisonous. Other snakes use different kinds of self-defense. The **pine snake ⑯** from North America squirts out horrible-smelling fluid when threatened, while the European **grass snake ⑰** turns upside down with its tongue hanging out and pretends to be dead. The South American **false water cobra ⑱** has a dangerous

bite, and it warns away enemies in the same way as a true cobra by widening its neck. In places with cold winters, snakes hide away and hibernate. Most hide on their own, but North American **garter snakes ⑲** gather together in hundreds in underground dens. They come to the surface in the spring and squirm in tangled masses as they fight for the chance to mate.

Crocodiles and alligators

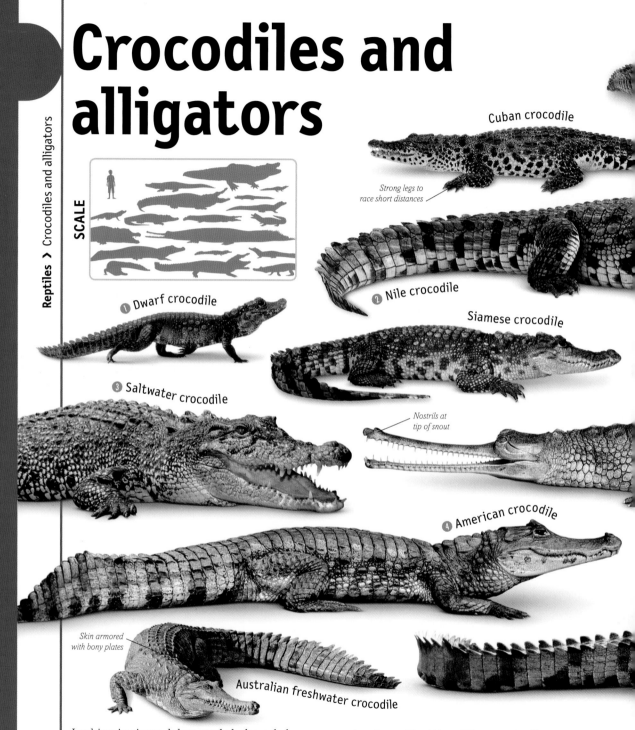

SCALE

Cuban crocodile

Strong legs to race short distances

① Dwarf crocodile

② Nile crocodile

Siamese crocodile

③ Saltwater crocodile

Nostrils at tip of snout

④ American crocodile

Skin armored with bony plates

Australian freshwater crocodile

Lurking in rivers, lakes, and sheltered shores, crocodiles and alligators use stealth and muscle power to ambush and kill their prey. Even the smallest kinds, such as the African **dwarf crocodile** ①, have scales like armor plating, while the largest can smash open boats with their giant jaws. Crocodiles swallow small animals whole. They tear bigger ones apart, after pulling them underwater so

they drown. The African **Nile crocodile** ② often lies in wait near the banks of rivers and water holes, where it attacks animals coming to drink. Females are devoted parents, guarding their eggs and carrying their young to water once they have hatched. Found in Australia and Southeast Asia, the **saltwater crocodile** ③ is the biggest reptile in the world. Measuring up to 23 ft (7 m) long, it is

5 American alligator

6 Chinese alligator

Cuvier's dwarf caiman

7 Broad-snouted caiman

Sharp teeth to tear prey apart

Orinoco crocodile

8 Spectacled caiman

9 Gharial

Schneider's dwarf caiman

Eyes high on head to spot prey from underwater

Yacare caiman

Marsh crocodile

Black caiman

a notorious man-eater, often attacking after dark. The **American crocodile 4** feeds mainly on fish, while the **American alligator 5** eats all kinds of animals, from frogs to deer. Like the rare **Chinese alligator 6**, it can be told from true crocodiles by the shape of its head, and by the way its teeth fit together when its mouth is closed. Caimans are relatives of alligators from Central and South America. The **broad-snouted caiman 7** lives in marshes and swamps, while the **spectacled caiman 8** lives on coasts, as well as in inland lakes and rivers. The critically endangered **gharial 9** is a unique fish-eating species from India, with extremely narrow jaws and dozens of sharply pointed teeth. It lives in deep rivers and finds its prey mainly by touch.

INDEX

ACKNOWLEDGMENTS

THE SMITHSONIAN INSTITUTION:

Project Coordinator: Kealy Wilson

Smithsonian Enterprises:
Kealy Wilson, Product Development Manager
Ellen Nanney, Licensing Manager
Brigid Ferraro, Director of Licensing
Carol LeBlanc, Senior Vice President

Reviewers for the National Zoo: Donald Moore III, Director, Animal Care Sciences, Scott R. Derrickson, Deputy Director, Smithsonian Conservation Biology Institute, Ed Bronikowski, Senior Curator, Tony Barthel, Curator, Elephant Trails, Asia Trail, and Cheetah Conservation Station, Alan Peters, Curator, Invertebrate Exhibit & Pollinarium, Bob King, Curator, Primates, Steven Sarro, Curator, Small Mammal House, Jim Murphy, Curator, Reptile Discovery Center, Craig Saffoe, Curator, Great Cats, Kids' Farm and Andean Bears, Frank Clements, Park Manager, Horticulture, Stacey Tabellario, Animal Keeper, Asia Trail, Juan Rodriguez, Animal Keeper, Asia Trail, Gil Myers, Animal Keeper, Cheetah Conservation Station, Kate Volz, Animal Keeper, Cheetah Conservation Station, Mike Henley, Biologist, Invertebrate Exhibit & Pollinarium, Donna Stockton, Biologist, Invertebrate Exhibit & Pollinarium, Michael Miller, Animal Keeper, Invertebrate Exhibit & Pollinarium, Erin Stromberg, Animal Keeper, Primates, Kenton Kerns, Animal Keeper, Small Mammal House, David Kessler, Animal Keeper, Small Mammal House, Rebecca Smithson, Animal Keeper, Small Mammal House, Sara Hallager, Animal Keeper, Bird House, Hillary Colton, Animal Keeper, Bird House, Lori Smith, Animal Keeper, Bird House, Debi Talbott, Animal Keeper, Bird House, Kathleen Brader, Animal Keeper, Bird House, Gwendolyn Cooper, Animal Keeper, Bird House, Warren Lynch, Animal Keeper, Smithsonian Conservation Biology Institute, Budhan Pukazhenthi, Reproductive Physiologist, Smithsonian Conservation Biology Institute, Peter Marra, Research Ecologist, Smithsonian Migratory Bird Center, Pamela Baker-Masson, Director, Communications, Jennifer Zoon, Communications Assistant, and special thanks to Susie Ellis.

Reviewers for the National Museum of Natural History: Dr Don W Wilson, Curator Emeritus, Department of Vertebrate Zoology, Dr Carole C Baldwin, Curator of Fishes, Lynne R Parenti, Curator of Fishes and Research Scientist, G David Johnson, Ichthyologist/Curator, Division of Fishes, Carla J Dove, PhD, Feather Identification Lab.

DK would like to thank:
Katie John for text assistance, Alison Gardner, Sunita Gahir, Konica Juneja, Kanika Mittal, Divya PR, and Upasana Sharma for design assistance, Hedi Hunter for design styling, Lili Bryant, Neha Chaudhary, Megha Gupta, Nandini Gupta, Suefa Lee, Vineetha Mokkil, Yamuna Matheswaran, and Rupa Rao for editorial assistance, Kealy Wilson and Ellen Nanney from the Smithsonian Institution, Angela Baynham for proofreading, Elizabeth Wise for the index.

The publisher would like to thank the following for their kind permission to reproduce their photographs:

(Key: a-above; b-below/bottom; c-center; f-far; l-left; r-right; t-top)

4-5 **Superstock:** Chris Mattison / age fotostock. 6 **Photoshot:** James Carmichael Jr (ca, bl). **Science Photo Library:** Dr.Morley Read (cla). 8 **Getty Images:** Photodisc / Life On White (cl); Purestock (clb). 9 **Corbis:** All Canada Photos / Jared Hobbs (crb). 10 **Corbis:** Minden Pictures / Piotr Naskrecki (tc). **Dreamstime.com:** Mgkuijpers (cr). **FLPA:** Imagebroker / Winfried Schäfer (clb); Photo Researchers (cra). **naturepl.com:** Michael D. Kern (bc). 11 **Corbis:** Minden Pictures / Stephen Dalton (c); Reuters / Jose Luis Saavedra (tc). **FLPA:** Minden Pictures / Michael & Patricia Fogden (tr); Minden Pictures / Piotr Naskrecki (tr). 12 **FLPA:** Photo Researchers (tr). **naturepl.com:** Nature Production (bl). **Science Photo Library:** Dante Fenolio (cb). 13 **Alamy Images:** Ladi Kirn (tr); Vibe Images / Jack Goldfarb (cr). **Corbis:** Minden Pictures / Pete Oxford (tl). **Dreamstime.com:** Jason P Ross (br). **Getty Images:** Visuals Unlimited, Inc. / Michael Redmer (crb). **naturepl.com:** Barry Mansell (cra). **Science Photo Library:**

E.R.Degginger (bc). 16-17 **Dreamstime.com:** Lloyd Luecke (tc). 16 **Corbis:** Minden Pictures / SA Team / Foto Natura (bl); David A. Northcott (br). **Dorling Kindersley:** Jerry Young (br). **Dreamstime.com:** Amwu (tc). 17 **Corbis:** Visuals Unlimited / Michael Redmer (cb). **Dreamstime.com:** Peter Leahy (crb). **Getty Images:** Visuals Unlimited, Inc. / Michael Redmer (ca). 18 **Dreamstime.com:** Checco (crb). 19 **Corbis:** Imagemore Co., Ltd (cb). **Dorling Kindersley:** Jerry Young (cr, cl, br). **Dreamstime.com:** Amwu (tla). 21 **Alamy Images:** Searagen (br). **Dorling Kindersley:** Jerry Young (crb). 22 **Getty Images:** Mint Images / Frans Lanting (c). **Photoshot:** A.N.T. Photo Library (tc); Ken Griffiths (ca). 24 **Alamy Images:** Michal Cerny (crb). **Corbis:** Auscape / Minden Pictures / Jean-Paul Ferrero (cr); David Northcott (cla). **Dorling Kindersley:** Diego Reggianti (cra). 25 **FLPA:** Minden Pictures / Mitsuhiko Imamori (clb); Minden Pictures / Michael & Patricia Fogden (crb). **Getty Images:** Joel Sartore (tl). 28 **Alamy Images:** Jan Csernoch (cb). **Dorling Kindersley:** Jerry Young (ca). **Dreamstime.com:** Nico Smit (bl). **Getty Images:** Minden Pictures / Mike Parry (cl). 28-29 **Photoshot:** Andrea & Antonella Ferrari (bc). 29 **Alamy Images:** Prisma Bildagentur AG / Dani Carlo (cla). **Corbis:** Minden Pictures / Pete Oxford (clb); Minden Pictures / Luciano Candisani (crb). **Dreamstime.com:** Lukas Blazek (c). **Getty Images:** Age Fotostock / Morales (br).

All other images © Dorling Kindersley
For further information see: www.dkimages.com